it had ❤ to be You

A COUPLE'S JOURNAL TO FILL WITH WORDS OF LOVE

ROCK
POINT

Brimming with creative inspiration, how-to projects, and useful information to enrich your everyday life, Quarto Knows is a favorite destination for those pursuing their interests and passions. Visit our site and dig deeper with our books into your area of interest: Quarto Creates, Quarto Cooks, Quarto Homes, Quarto Lives, Quarto Drives, Quarto Explores, Quarto Gifts, or Quarto Kids.

10 9 8 7 6 5 4 3 2 1

ISBN: 978-1-63106-451-7

Editorial Director: Rage Kindelsperger
Senior Editor: Erin Canning
Managing Editor: Cara Donaldson
Cover and Interior Design: Tandem Books

Printed in China

Image Credits
Cover: purple backgound © Alexander_Evgenyevic/Shutterstock, heart on back cover © Zukerman/Shutterstock, heart on cover and spine © zsooofija/Shutterstock, foil texture on spine © detchana wangkheeree/Shutterstock.

Interior: White title heart © zsooofija/Shutterstock, lavender background © Luria/Shutterstock, cool colors watercolor texture © wrongorright/Shutterstock, watercolor edges © Evgenia L/Shutterstock, Red watercolor texture © goldnetz/Shutterstock, pink watercolor texture © Lyubov Tolstova/Shutterstock, blue watercolor texture © Luria/Shutterstock, pink to orange ombre watercolor texture © Angie Makes/Shutterstock, line hearts © iktash/Shutterstock, pink and orange watercolor teture © TairA/Shutterstock, white watercolor heart © Maria Zvonkova/Shutterstock, small hearts © Natasha Zalevskaya/Shutterstock, notebook shape © OnD/Shutterstock, bright watercolor texture © Rolau Elena/Shutterstock, pink to white ombre watercolor texture © switzergirl/Shutterstock, and large purple heart © ghenadie/Shutterstock.

Please note that while we have tried our best to make all facts present in this book as accurate as possible, The Quarto Group and its employees cannot be held liable for any errors, omissions, or inconsistences.

An Introduction to Us 4

Before You 7

Then There Was You 25

All about Us 43

All about You 55

Between Us 69

The Best Is Yet to Come 79

AN INTRODUCTION TO US

There are countless reasons why it had to be you—
why it had to be us—from our childhood dreams about
the person we'd one day be with to all the twists and
turns that brought us together. Incalculable forces
brought us together, and now, nothing can keep us
apart. This journal is the story of us—who we were,
who we are, and who we hope to be one day. It will
explore and celebrate our love, as we write about
each other and our shared experiences.

How to Use This Journal

Each of you gets a heart, one of you pink and
one of you red. When there's one heart at the
top of a page, the person with that color heart
writes on that page. When the hearts are
joined, write together.

This journal belongs to

pink heart _____

red heart _&_ Melvin

Love can only be found through the act of loving.

— PAULO COELHO

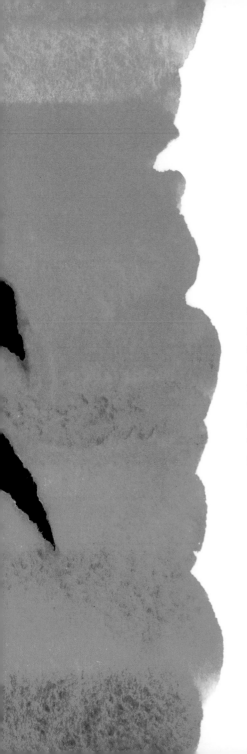

Before You

Once upon a time we were children. We had lives separate from each other, as hard as that is to imagine now. The paths we were on turned us into the people we are today—and converged to bring us together. But before you . . .

♥ WHEN I WAS A KID, I IMAGINED MY TRUE LOVE WOULD BE . . .

♥ I KNEW I WOULD END UP WITH SOMEONE LIKE YOU, WHO . . .

_____

_____

_____

_____

_____

_____

_____

_____

_____

♥ I NEVER THOUGHT I WOULD END UP WITH SOMEONE LIKE
YOU, WHO . . .

_____

_____

_____

_____

_____

_____

_____

_____

_____

♥ I believe . . .

in fate.

◯ yes

◯ no

in love at first sight.

◯ yes

◯ no

opposites attract.

◯ yes

◯ no

in soul mates.

◯ yes

◯ no

love conquers all.

◯ yes

◯ no

you have to love yourself
in order to be loved.

◯ yes

◯ no

love is infinite.

◯ yes

◯ no

I believe . . .

in fate.

☑ yes

☐ no

in love at first sight.

☑ yes

☐ no

opposites attract.

☑ yes

☐ no

in soul mates.

☑ yes

☐ no

love conquers all.

☑ yes

☐ no

you have to love yourself
in order to be loved.

☑ yes

☐ no

love is infinite.

☑ yes

☐ no

💜 IF THIS HAD HAPPENED, WE WOULD HAVE NEVER MET . . .

💜 BEFORE WE MET, I WAS SURE THAT . . .

💜 IF THIS HAD HAPPENED, WE WOULD HAVE NEVER MET . . .

....

....

....

....

....

....

....

....

....

💜 BEFORE WE MET, I WAS SURE THAT . . .

....

....

....

....

....

....

....

....

....

....

....

♥ Write a love poem for your partner.

♥ *Write a love poem for your partner.*

I Pause, Body frozen mind
Searching...。

Something Seems to be pulling
me...I Search and find this
Glow

What is it?
eyes trying to focus, nothing
is clear, nothing makes sense.

My heart is Racing. My stomach
feels different. theres a Rush
of Energy entering my mind

What is happening?

the picture get clear. Her eyes
Her Smile they have me locked.

Please don't let me Go. I want
to be here forever.

♥ MY FAVORITE THING ABOUT BEING SINGLE WAS . . .

♥ MY LEAST FAVORITE THING ABOUT BEING SINGLE WAS . . .

♥ MY FAVORITE THING ABOUT BEING SINGLE WAS . . .

♥ MY LEAST FAVORITE THING ABOUT BEING SINGLE WAS . . .

♥ RIGHT BEFORE WE MET, I WAS . . .

♥ RIGHT BEFORE WE MET, I WAS . . .

Relationship Wit & Wisdom

- NEVER GO TO BED ANGRY.

- ONLY WHEN THE RIGHT PERSON COMES ALONG CAN YOU FINALLY SEE WHY ALL THE OTHERS WERE WRONG.

- ABSENCE MAKES THE HEART GROW FONDER.

 My own wit and wisdom:

• YOU CAN'T RUSH SOMETHING THAT YOU WANT
TO LAST FOREVER.

• HAPPINESS IS AN INSIDE JOB.

• DON'T WAIT TO TALK—LISTEN.

• TRY TO UNDERSTAND INSTEAD OF TRYING TO CONVINCE.

• BE PATIENT WITH LOVE'S CYCLES—NO FLOWER
BLOOMS YEAR-ROUND.

My own wit and wisdom:

They gave each other a smile with a future in it.

— RING LARDNER

Then There Was You

When we met, a new chapter in our lives began. We were starting on a path to something big, something amazing, something that would last our lifetimes.

I was once alone, but then there was you . . .

 WE MET WHEN . . .

♥ WE MET WHEN. . .

 THE VERY FIRST TIME I SAW YOU, I THOUGHT . . .

♥ THE VERY FIRST TIME I SAW YOU, I THOUGHT . . .

♥ *Draw a picture from early in your relationship.*

♥ **Draw a picture from early in your relationship.**

OUR FIRST DATE WAS . . .

THE BEST PART OF THE DATE WAS . . .

♥ AFTER OUR FIRST DATE, I THOUGHT . . .

_____

_____

_____

_____

_____

_____

_____

_____

♥ AFTER OUR FIRST DATE, I THOUGHT . . .

_____

_____

_____

_____

_____

_____

_____

_____

_____

♥ IF I COULD GO BACK IN TIME AND GIVE MYSELF ADVICE BEFORE OUR
FIRST DATE, I WOULD TELL MYSELF . . .

_____

_____

_____

_____

_____

_____

_____

_____

♥ IF I COULD GO BACK IN TIME AND GIVE YOU ADVICE BEFORE OUR
FIRST DATE, I WOULD TELL YOU . . .

_____

_____

_____

_____

_____

_____

_____

_____

_____

♥ IF I COULD GO BACK IN TIME AND GIVE MYSELF ADVICE BEFORE OUR
FIRST DATE, I WOULD TELL MYSELF . . .

....

....

....

....

....

....

....

....

♥ IF I COULD GO BACK IN TIME AND GIVE YOU ADVICE BEFORE OUR
FIRST DATE, I WOULD TELL YOU . . .

....

....

....

....

....

....

....

....

....

♥ WHEN WE FIRST STARTED DATING, I WAS SURE THAT . . .

♥ WHEN WE FIRST STARTED DATING, I WAS SURE THAT . . .

Doodle Your Hearts Out

Doodling hearts with your initials in them is a classic way to say "I love you." Doodle some messages for each other here.

♥ I KNEW I LOVED YOU WHEN . . .

_____

_____

_____

_____

_____

_____

_____

_____

♥ I KNEW I LOVED YOU WHEN . . .

_____

_____

_____

_____

_____

_____

_____

_____

_____

_____

THE FIRST TIME WE SAID "I LOVE YOU" . . .

WE COMMITTED TO EACH OTHER WHEN . . .

Love does not consist in gazing at each other, but in looking together in the same direction.

— ANTOINE DE SAINT-EXUPÉRY

All about Us

Our life together has been an amazing adventure! The ups are higher and the downs are cushioned because of our love. Someone should write a love story all about us . . .

OUR BEST DATE (SO FAR) WAS . . .

OUR FIRST BIG RELATIONSHIP STEP WAS . . .

THE FUNNIEST THING THAT HAS HAPPENED TO US IS . . .

THE HARDEST THING WE'VE BEEN THROUGH IS . . .

OUR FIRST BIG FIGHT WAS . . .

WE MADE UP BY . . .

Anniversaries

We met
_____

Our first date
_____

We committed to
each other/
got married
_____

Our first kiss
_____

Our best anniversary so far:

_____

_____

_____

_____

_____

Favorites

Our favorite movie
_____

Our favorite song
_____

Our favorite place
_____

Our favorite meal
_____

Our favorite thing about us:

_____
_____
_____
_____
_____

WHEN WE WORK TOGETHER, WE'RE BEST AT . . .

THE GREATEST THING WE'VE ACCOMPLISHED TOGETHER IS . . .

OUR FIRST TRIP TOGETHER WAS . . .

THE BEST MEAL WE'VE HAD IS . . .

THINGS WE LIKE TO DO ON A QUIET NIGHT IN ARE . . .

WHEN WE WANT TO PAINT THE TOWN RED, WE . . .

💕 THE BIGGEST THING WE HAVE IN COMMON IS . . .

💕 THE BIGGEST DIFFERENCE BETWEEN US IS . . .

The greatest happiness of life is the conviction that we are loved; loved for ourselves, or rather, loved in spite of ourselves.

—VICTOR HUGO

All about You

From our uncanny similarities to our biggest differences, there are at least a million reasons why we love each other. That's why this chapter is all about you . . .

♥ MY FAVORITE THING THAT YOU DO IS . . .

_____

_____

_____

_____

_____

_____

_____

_____

_____

♥ I COULDN'T LIVE WITHOUT YOUR . . .

_____

_____

_____

_____

_____

_____

_____

_____

_____

_____

_____

♥ MY FAVORITE THING THAT YOU DO IS . . .

♥ I COULDN'T LIVE WITHOUT YOUR . . .

My Love Letter to

Dear _____,

Love,

_____

My Love Letter to

Dear _____,

Love,

_____

♥ MY FAVORITE PART OF YOUR BODY IS . . .

♥ YOU GIVE ME GOOSE BUMPS WHEN . . .

♥ MY FAVORITE PART OF YOUR BODY IS . . .

_____

_____

_____

_____

_____

_____

_____

_____

_____

♥ YOU GIVE ME GOOSE BUMPS WHEN . . .

_____

_____

_____

_____

_____

_____

_____

_____

_____

_____

♥ YOU AMAZE ME WHEN . . .

♥ YOU'VE INSPIRED ME TO . . .

♥ YOU AMAZE ME WHEN . . .

♥ YOU'VE INSPIRED ME TO . . .

 # Fill in the Love.

When you _____, my heart beats faster.

Your eyes are _____.

My favorite quirk of yours is _____.

I can never get enough of your _____.

Every time you _____, I feel weak in the knees.

I remember when you told me _____.

I hope you will always _____.

Your _____ is the absolute best!

My biggest wish for you is _____.

Every time you _____, I am always impressed.

I laugh every time you _____.

I love to watch you _____.

You remind me of the superhero _____ because
_____.

I wish I could _____ like you.

You are my _____ and my _____.

Fill in the Love.

When you _____, my heart beats faster.

Your eyes are _____.

My favorite quirk of yours is _____.

I can never get enough of your _____.

Every time you _____, I feel weak in the knees.

I remember when you told me _____.

I hope you will always _____.

Your _____ is the absolute best!

My biggest wish for you is _____.

Every time you _____, I am always impressed.

I laugh every time you _____.

I love to watch you _____.

You remind me of the superhero _____ because
_____.

I wish I could _____ like you.

You are my _____ and my _____.

♥ YOU'VE TAUGHT ME TO . . .

♥ I CAN ALWAYS COUNT ON YOU TO . . .

♥ YOU'VE TAUGHT ME TO . . .

♥ I CAN ALWAYS COUNT ON YOU TO . . .

I love you and I like you.

— LESLIE KNOPE,
PARKS AND RECREATION

Between Us

We share so many deep
secrets, inside jokes, daily
habits, and little rituals that
make our lives together rich
and full of love. But all that
stuff is just between us . . .

♥ THE CUTEST THING YOU DO THAT ONLY I KNOW ABOUT IS . . .

....

....

....

....

....

....

....

....

....

♥ I WOULD NEVER TELL ANYONE BUT YOU THAT . . .

....

....

....

....

....

....

....

....

....

....

....

♥ THE CUTEST THING YOU DO THAT ONLY I KNOW ABOUT IS . . .

....

....

....

....

....

....

....

....

....

♥ I WOULD NEVER TELL ANYONE BUT YOU THAT . . .

....

....

....

....

....

....

....

....

....

....

....

OUR BEST INSIDE JOKES ARE . . .

WE RELAX TOGETHER BY . . .

OUR FAVORITE DAILY RITUALS ARE . . .

Our Secret Language

We know each other so well, we can communicate by just a look or code word that only we understand. Here's our codebook.

I love you! _____

You are so adorable! _____

I want you! _____

You are hilarious! _____

I completely agree. _____

Relax; there's nothing we can do about it.
_____

Be careful with what you say next. _____

I'm fine. _____

Save me! _____

I need some reassurance. _____

You're my favorite person ever. _____

Let's get out of here soon. _____

We're leaving right now. _____

I can't believe this is happening! _____

I'm starving! _____

You can eat the last one. _____

You better not eat the last one! _____

Let's buy this one. _____

Let's not get anything at this place. _____

Can you believe this guy/gal?! _____

I need help with this. _____

Let's go help that person. _____

Let's avoid that person. _____

OUR BEST CONVERSATIONS ARE USUALLY ABOUT . . .

WE REALLY GET EACH OTHER WHEN IT COMES TO . . .

♥♥ OUR FAVORITE THINGS TO DO WHEN IT'S JUST US ARE . . .

♥♥ THE MOST SPECIAL, PRIVATE MOMENT WE'VE SHARED IS . . .

The heart that has truly
loved never forgets,
But as truly loves on
to the close.

—THOMAS MOORE

The Best Is Yet to Come

We love each other more and more all the time. Every day that goes by, our devotion grows, as does our enjoyment of each other. That's how we know that the best is yet to come . . .

♥ I CAN'T WAIT TO DO THIS WITH YOU . . .

I CAN'T WAIT TO DO THIS WITH YOU . . .

OUR NEXT BIG ADVENTURE WILL BE . . .

IF WE COULD GO ANYWHERE IN THE WORLD, WE'D . . .

💕 IF WE WON THE LOTTERY TOMORROW, WE'D . . .

💕 WE CAN'T WAIT UNTIL WE . . .

Our Bucket List

There is so much we can't wait to do together!

Places to go:

1.
2.
3.
4.
5.
6.
7.
8.
9.
10.

Things to learn:

1.
2.
3.
4.
5.
6.
7.
8.
9.
10.

Things to try:

1.
2.
3.
4.
5.
6.
7.
8.
9.
10.

Goals to meet:

1.
2.
3.
4.
5.
6.
7.
8.
9.
10.

THE NEXT TIME WE ARGUE, INSTEAD OF DOING WHAT I USUALLY DO, I'LL . . .

♥ THE NEXT TIME WE ARGUE, INSTEAD OF DOING WHAT I USUALLY DO, I'LL . . .

THE NEXT THING WE WILL DO FOR OUR HOME WILL BE . . .

THE NEXT THING WE WILL CREATE TOGETHER WILL BE . . .

 WE'VE ALWAYS TALKED ABOUT DOING THIS,
SO LET'S . . .

FOR OUR NEXT ANNIVERSARY, LET'S . . .

To the Future Us

Here are some words of advice, hopes, and memories we will always treasure.

We hope we always:

....

....

....

....

....

Let's never forget:

....

....

....

....

....

Our best advice for future us:

....

....

....

....

....

Our favorite memory so far:

_____

_____

_____

_____

_____

Our fondest wish for the future:

_____

_____

_____

_____

_____

The way we feel right at this moment:

_____

_____

_____

_____

_____

♥ IN FIVE YEARS, I THINK WE'LL . . .

♥ IN TWENTY YEARS, I THINK WE'LL . . .

♥ IN FIVE YEARS, I THINK WE'LL . . .

♥ IN TWENTY YEARS, I THINK WE'LL . . .

WHEN I THINK ABOUT WHAT YOU'LL BE LIKE IN THE FUTURE,
I IMAGINE . . .

♥ WHEN I THINK ABOUT WHAT YOU'LL BE LIKE IN THE FUTURE,
I IMAGINE . . .

The loving are the daring.

— BAYARD TAYLOR